Learn Python

Practical Guide

A. De Quattro

Copyright © 2024

Python guide

1.Introduction to Python programming language

Python is a high-level programming language that is widely used for various purposes such as web development, data analysis, artificial intelligence, scientific computing, and more. It was created by Guido van Rossum in the late 1980s and has since become one of the most popular programming languages worldwide.

One of the main reasons for Python's popularity is its simplicity and readability. The syntax of Python is clean and easy to understand, making it an excellent language for beginners to learn. It also has a large standard library that includes modules and packages for a wide range of tasks, reducing the need for developers to write code from scratch.

Python is an interpreted language, which means that code is executed line by line by the

Python interpreter. This allows for quick prototyping and debugging, making Python a great choice for developing applications rapidly. Additionally, Python is platform-independent, meaning that code written in Python can run on any operating system without modification.

Another key feature of Python is its strong support for object-oriented programming. Objects in Python have attributes and methods that can be accessed and modified, allowing for the creation of reusable and modular code. Python also supports functional programming, allowing developers to write code in a more declarative and concise manner.

Python has a large and active community of developers who contribute to the language's development and maintain numerous libraries and frameworks. This vast ecosystem of third-party libraries and tools makes Python extremely versatile and powerful. Some popular libraries include NumPy for scientific computing, Pandas for data manipulation, Django for web development, and TensorFlow for machine learning.

In recent years, Python has become the go-to language for machine learning and artificial intelligence applications. Its simple syntax and extensive libraries have made it a popular choice for developing models and algorithms for data analysis, natural language processing, image recognition, and more.

Overall, Python is a versatile and powerful programming language that is well-suited for a wide range of applications. Whether you are a beginner looking to learn your first programming language or an experienced developer working on complex projects, Python is a great choice due to its simplicity, readability, and robustness. If you haven't already, I highly recommend giving Python a try and exploring its vast potential for your coding needs.

2.Installing Python on your computer

Python is a high-level programming language that is widely used for various purposes such as web development, data analysis, artificial intelligence, scientific computing, and more. It was created by Guido van Rossum in the late 1980s and has since become one of the most popular programming languages worldwide.

One of the main reasons for Python's popularity is its simplicity and readability. The syntax of Python is clean and easy to understand, making it an excellent language for beginners to learn. It also has a large standard library that includes modules and packages for a wide range of tasks, reducing the need for developers to write code from scratch.

Python is an interpreted language, which means that code is executed line by line by the Python interpreter. This allows for quick prototyping and debugging, making Python a great choice for developing applications rapidly. Additionally, Python is platform-independent, meaning that code written in Python can run on any operating system without modification.

Another key feature of Python is its strong support for object-oriented programming. Objects in Python have attributes and methods that can be accessed and modified, allowing for the creation of reusable and modular code. Python also supports functional programming, allowing developers to write code in a more declarative and concise manner.

Python has a large and active community of developers who contribute to the language's development and maintain numerous libraries and frameworks. This vast ecosystem of third-party libraries and tools makes Python extremely versatile and powerful. Some popular libraries include NumPy for scientific computing, Pandas for data manipulation,

Django for web development, and TensorFlow for machine learning.

In recent years, Python has become the go-to language for machine learning and artificial intelligence applications. Its simple syntax and extensive libraries have made it a popular choice for developing models and algorithms for data analysis, natural language processing, image recognition, and more.

Overall, Python is a versatile and powerful programming language that is well-suited for a wide range of applications. Whether you are a beginner looking to learn your first programming language or an experienced developer working on complex projects, Python is a great choice due to its simplicity, readability, and robustness. If you haven't already, I highly recommend giving Python a try and exploring its vast potential for your coding needs.

3.Basic syntax and data types in Python

Python is a high-level programming language known for its simplicity and readability. In this article, we will discuss the basic syntax and data types in Python to help beginners get started with programming in this versatile language.

Python uses indentation to define blocks of code, unlike other languages that use braces or keywords. This makes the code easier to read and understand. Statements that belong to the same block must have the same indentation level. For example, a block of code inside a function definition would have a consistent indentation level.

Here is an example of a simple Python function:

```python
```

```
def greet(name):
    print("Hello, " + name + "!")
```

In this example, the `def` keyword is used to define a function called `greet`, which takes a parameter `name`. The `print` statement inside the function is indented to indicate that it belongs to the `greet` function.

Python is dynamically typed, which means that you do not have to specify variable types when declaring them. Variables are automatically assigned a type based on the value they are assigned. You can use the `type()` function to check the type of a variable.

```python
x = 10
y = "Hello"
```

```
print(type(x))  # <class 'int'>
print(type(y))  # <class 'str'>
```

Python has several built-in data types, including integers, floats, strings, booleans, lists, tuples, sets, and dictionaries. Let's take a closer look at each of these data types:

1. Integers: Integers are whole numbers without decimal points.

```python
x = 10
```

2. Floats: Floats are numbers with decimal points.

```python
y = 3.14
```

3. Strings: Strings are sequences of characters enclosed in single or double quotes.

```python
name = "Alice"
```

4. Booleans: Booleans represent truth values (True or False).

```python
is_valid = True
```

5. Lists: Lists are ordered collections of items.

```python
numbers = [1, 2, 3, 4, 5]
```

6. Tuples: Tuples are ordered collections that are immutable (cannot be modified).

```python
coordinates = (10, 20)
```

7. Sets: Sets are unordered collections of unique elements.

```python
```

```
fruits = {"apple", "banana", "cherry"}
```

8. Dictionaries: Dictionaries are collections of key-value pairs.

```python
person = {"name": "Alice", "age": 30}
```

Python also supports type conversion, allowing you to convert variables from one type to another. This can be done using specific functions such as `int()`, `float()`, `str()`, `list()`, `tuple()`, `set()`, and `dict()`.

```python
x = 10
y = float(x)
```

```

Python also has operators for performing arithmetic, comparison, logical, and bitwise operations. Here are some common operators in Python:

- Arithmetic operators: `+`, `-`, `*`, `/`, `//` (floor division), `%` (modulo), `**` (exponentiation)

- Comparison operators: `==` (equal), `!=` (not equal), `<`, `>`, `<=`, `>=`

- Logical operators: `and`, `or`, `not`

- Bitwise operators: `&` (AND), `|` (OR), `^` (XOR), `~` (NOT), `<<` (left shift), `>>` (right shift)

```python
x = 10
y = 20

```python
print(x + y)   # 30
print(x == y)  # False
print(x < y)   # True
print(not (x > y))  # True
```

Python also provides control flow statements such as `if`, `elif`, `else`, `for`, `while`, and `break` to control the flow of execution in a program. These statements allow you to make decisions, iterate over sequences, and break out of loops based on certain conditions.

```python
score = 85

if score >= 90:
    print("Grade A")
```

```
elif score >= 80:
    print("Grade B")
else:
    print("Grade C")
```

Functions in Python allow you to encapsulate and reuse code. You can define a function using the `def` keyword and call it with the appropriate arguments. Functions can return values using the `return` statement.

```python
def add(x, y):
    return x + y


result = add(10, 20)
print(result)  # 30
```

Python also has built-in functions for performing common operations, such as `len()`, `range()`, `sum()`, `max()`, `min()`, `sorted()`, and `zip()`.

```python
numbers = [1, 2, 3, 4, 5]

print(len(numbers))  # 5
print(sum(numbers))  # 15
print(max(numbers))  # 5
print(min(numbers))  # 1
```

In addition to the built-in functions, Python has a rich standard library with modules for performing more advanced tasks, such as working with files, networking, databases, and data processing.

Python also supports the concept of modules and packages, allowing you to organize code into reusable components. You can create modules by writing Python code in separate `.py` files and import them into your main program using the `import` statement.

```python
# module.py
def greet(name):
    print("Hello, " + name + "!")

# main.py
import module

module.greet("Alice")
```

Python is a versatile language that is widely used in various fields, including web development, data science, machine learning, artificial intelligence, and automation. It has a large and active community of developers who contribute to its growth and popularity.

Python's basic syntax and data types are easy to learn and understand, making it an excellent choice for beginners in programming. By mastering these fundamental concepts, you can build a solid foundation for further exploration and growth in Python development.

4. Operators and expressions in Python

Operators and expressions are fundamental concepts in any programming language, including Python. They are used to manipulate values and variables to perform various operations, such as arithmetic calculations, logical comparisons, and bitwise operations.

In Python, operators are symbols that represent specific operations, such as addition (+), subtraction (-), multiplication (*), division (/), and many others. They are used to perform operations on operands, which can be variables, constants, or values.

Expressions in Python are combinations of variables, operators, and constants that produce a value when evaluated. An expression can be as simple as a single variable or as complex as a combination of multiple operators and operands. Expressions can be used in assignments, function calls, conditional statements, loops, and many other places in Python code.

In Python, operators can be categorized into several types based on their functionality. Some of the common types of operators in Python include:

1. Arithmetic operators: These operators are used to perform arithmetic calculations, such as addition, subtraction, multiplication, division, and modulus. The arithmetic operators in Python are + (addition), - (subtraction), * (multiplication), / (division), and % (modulus).

2. Comparison operators: Comparison operators are used to compare two values and determine whether one value is greater than, less than, equal to, or not equal to another value. Some of the comparison operators in Python include < (less than), > (greater than), == (equal to), != (not equal to), <= (less than

or equal to), and >= (greater than or equal to).

3. Logical operators: Logical operators are used to combine multiple conditions and determine the truth value of a compound expression. The logical operators in Python include and (logical AND), or (logical OR), and not (logical NOT).

4. Bitwise operators: Bitwise operators are used to perform bitwise operations on integers. These operators manipulate individual bits of integers and perform operations such as AND, OR, XOR, left shift, and right shift. Some of the bitwise operators in Python include & (bitwise AND), | (bitwise OR), ^ (bitwise XOR), << (left shift), and >> (right shift).

5. Assignment operators: Assignment operators are used to assign a value to a variable. The most common assignment operator in Python is =, which assigns the

value on the right side of the operator to the variable on the left side. Other assignment operators include += (addition assignment), -= (subtraction assignment), *= (multiplication assignment), /= (division assignment), and %= (modulus assignment).

6. Identity operators: Identity operators are used to determine whether two variables refer to the same object in memory. The identity operators in Python are is (returns True if two variables refer to the same object) and is not (returns True if two variables do not refer to the same object).

7. Membership operators: Membership operators are used to test whether a value is present in a sequence, such as a list, tuple, or string. The membership operators in Python are in (returns True if a value is present in a sequence) and not in (returns True if a value is not present in a sequence).

8. Unary operators: Unary operators act on only one operand and perform operations such as negation, logical inversion, and bitwise inversion. The unary operators in Python include - (negation), not (logical inversion), and ~ (bitwise inversion).

In Python, operators have precedence levels that determine the order in which operators are evaluated in an expression. Operators with higher precedence levels are evaluated before operators with lower precedence levels. For example, multiplication and division operators have a higher precedence level than addition and subtraction operators, so they are evaluated first in an expression.

In addition to precedence levels, Python also supports associativity, which determines the order in which operators of the same precedence level are evaluated. Most operators in Python are left-associative, which means they are evaluated from left to right. However, some operators, such as the exponentiation operator (**), are right-associative and are evaluated from right to left.

Python also provides the ability to override operator precedence and associativity using parentheses in expressions. By using parentheses, you can control the order in which operators are evaluated and ensure that expressions are evaluated in the correct order.

Expressions in Python can be simple or complex, depending on the combination of operators and operands used. Simple expressions may consist of a single variable, constant, or function call, while complex expressions may involve multiple operators and operands connected by parentheses and other syntactic elements.

Here are some examples of expressions in Python:

1. Simple arithmetic expression:

x = 10

y = 5

z = x + y

In this example, the expression x + y calculates the sum of the variables x and y and assigns the result to the variable z.

2. Complex arithmetic expression:

x = 10

y = 5

z = (x + y) * 2

In this example, the expression (x + y) * 2 calculates the sum of the variables x and y and multiplies the result by 2. The final result is assigned to the variable z.

3. Logical expression:

x = 10

y = 5

print(x > y and x != y)

In this example, the expression x > y and x != y evaluates to True because both conditions are satisfied.

4. Bitwise expression:

x = 10

y = 5

print(x & y)

In this example, the expression x & y performs a bitwise AND operation on the binary representations of the variables x and y.

Overall, operators and expressions are essential concepts in Python programming that allow you to manipulate values, variables, and data structures to perform various operations. By understanding how operators work and how expressions are evaluated, you can write more efficient and concise Python code.

5. Control flow statements: if, else, elif, loops in Python

Control flow statements are critical components of any programming language, as they allow you to dictate the flow of your code based on certain conditions or criteria. In Python, there are several control flow statements that are commonly used, including if, else, elif, and loops. These statements help you make decisions in your code and execute certain blocks of code based on the outcome of those decisions.

The if statement is one of the most fundamental control flow statements in Python. It allows you to execute a block of code only if a certain condition is true. The basic syntax of an if statement in Python is as follows:

```python
```

```
if condition:
    # execute this block of code if the condition is true
```

Here's an example of how you can use an if statement in Python:

```python
x = 10

if x > 5:
    print("x is greater than 5")
```

In this example, the condition `x > 5` evaluates to true because the value of `x` is 10, which is indeed greater than 5. As a result, the statement "x is greater than 5" will be printed to the console.

In addition to the if statement, Python also provides the else statement, which allows you to execute a block of code if the condition specified in the if statement is false. Here's an example:

```python
x = 10

if x > 100:
    print("x is greater than 100")
else:
    print("x is not greater than 100")
```

In this example, since the condition `x > 100` evaluates to false, the code block under the else statement will be executed, and the message "x is not greater than 100" will be printed.

Sometimes, you may have multiple conditions that you want to check for. In such cases, you can use the elif statement, which stands for "else if". The elif statement allows you to specify additional conditions to check if the condition in the preceding if statement is false. Here's an example:

```python
x = 10

if x > 100:
    print("x is greater than 100")
elif x > 50:
    print("x is greater than 50 but less than 100")
```

else:

    print("x is less than or equal to 50")
```

In this example, the Python interpreter will first check if `x > 100`. Since this condition is false, it will then move on to the next condition specified in the elif statement, which is `x > 50`. Since `x` is equal to 10, this condition is also false, and the interpreter will execute the code block under the else statement, which prints "x is less than or equal to 50".

Another important aspect of control flow in Python is the concept of loops. Loops allow you to execute a block of code multiple times, either for a certain number of iterations or until a certain condition is met. There are two main types of loops in Python: the for loop and the while loop.
```

The for loop is used when you know the number of times you want to iterate over a block of code. Here's an example of how you can use a for loop in Python:

```python
for i in range(5):
    print(i)
```

In this example, the `range(5)` function generates a sequence of numbers from 0 to 4. The for loop then iterates over each number in this sequence and prints it to the console. The output of this code will be:

```
0
1
2
```

3
4
```

You can also iterate over other types of sequences using a for loop, such as lists or strings. Here's an example:

```python
fruits = ["apple", "banana", "cherry"]

for fruit in fruits:
    print(fruit)
```

In this example, the for loop iterates over each element in the `fruits` list and prints it to the console. The output of this code will be:
```

```
apple
banana
cherry
```

The while loop, on the other hand, is used when you want to iterate over a block of code until a certain condition is met. Here's an example of how you can use a while loop in Python:

```python
x = 0

while x < 5:
    print(x)
    x += 1
```

In this example, the while loop will continue to execute the block of code as long as the condition `x < 5` is true. The variable `x` is incremented by 1 in each iteration, so the output of this code will be:

```
0
1
2
3
4
```

It's important to be cautious when using while loops, as they can potentially result in an infinite loop if the condition specified never becomes false. To avoid this, make sure that the condition is updated within the loop, so that it eventually becomes false and the loop terminates.

In addition to the basic for and while loops, Python also provides the ability to use loop control statements such as `break` and `continue` to modify the behavior of loops. The `break` statement is used to exit a loop prematurely, while the `continue` statement is used to skip the rest of the current iteration and move on to the next iteration. Here's an example of how you can use these statements in a loop:

```python
for i in range(10):
    if i == 5:
        break
    if i % 2 == 0:
        continue
    print(i)
```

```

In this example, the loop will iterate over the numbers from 0 to 9. When `i` is equal to 5, the `break` statement will be executed, causing the loop to exit prematurely. If `i` is an even number, the `continue` statement will be executed, skipping the rest of the current iteration. The output of this code will be:

```
1
3
7
9
```

In conclusion, control flow statements such as if, else, elif, and loops are essential tools in Python that allow you to make decisions in
```

your code and control the flow of execution. By understanding how these statements work and practicing using them in your code, you can become a more proficient Python programmer and create more complex and efficient programs.

6. Functions in Python

Functions in Python are blocks of code that perform a specific task. They allow code to be organized into reusable modules, making the program easier to read, understand, and maintain. Functions are defined using the "def" keyword, followed by the function name, parentheses, and a colon.

Here is an example of a simple function in Python:

```python
def say_hello():
    print("Hello, world!")

say_hello()
```

In this example, the `say_hello()` function prints the message "Hello, world!" when called. Functions can also take parameters, which are values passed to the function when it is called.

```python
def greet(name):
    print("Hello, " + name + "!")

greet("Alice")
```

In this example, the `greet()` function takes a parameter `name`, and prints a personalized greeting using that parameter. Functions can also return values using the `return` statement.

```python
def add(a, b):
```

```
    return a + b


result = add(3, 5)

print(result)
```

In this example, the `add()` function takes two parameters `a` and `b`, and returns the sum of those two numbers. The `return` statement allows the function to pass a value back to the calling code.

Functions can also have default parameter values, which are used when a value is not provided by the calling code.

```python
def calculate_area(length, width=5):
    return length * width
```

```
print(calculate_area(3)) # Output: 15
print(calculate_area(3, 4)) # Output: 12
```

In this example, the `calculate_area()` function calculates the area of a rectangle using the provided length and width parameters. If the width parameter is not provided, it defaults to 5.

Python also supports lambda functions, which are small, anonymous functions defined using the `lambda` keyword.

```python
square = lambda x: x**2
print(square(3)) # Output: 9
```

Lambda functions are useful for creating simple, one-line functions without defining a separate function name. They can be used when passing functions as arguments to other functions, like `map()` or `filter()`.

Functions can also be nested, meaning a function is defined inside another function.

```python
def outer_function():

    def inner_function():
        print("This is the inner function")

    print("This is the outer function")
    inner_function()
```

outer_function()
```

In this example, the `inner_function()` is defined inside the `outer_function()`. Nested functions can access variables from the outer function, but the reverse is not true.

Python also supports recursive functions, which are functions that call themselves recursively until a base case is reached.

```python
def factorial(n):
    if n == 0:
        return 1
    return n * factorial(n-1)

print(factorial(5)) # Output: 120
```
```

```

In this example, the `factorial()` function calculates the factorial of a number using recursion. The base case is when `n == 0`, at which point the function returns 1.

Functions in Python can also have global and local variables. Global variables are declared outside of any function, and can be accessed from any function within the program. Local variables are declared inside a function, and can only be accessed within that function.

```python
global_var = 10

def my_function():
    local_var = 20
    print(global_var)

```
    print(local_var)

my_function()

print(global_var)

print(local_var) # This will raise an error
```

In this example, `global_var` is a global variable that can be accessed from within the `my_function()`. `local_var`, on the other hand, is a local variable that can only be accessed within the `my_function()`.

Python also supports the concept of scope, which defines where a variable can be accessed within a program. The scope of a variable is determined by where it is declared, with global variables having a global scope, and local variables having a local scope.

```python
x = 10

def my_function():
    x = 20
    print(x)

my_function()
print(x)
```

In this example, the `x` variable inside `my_function()` has a local scope and does not affect the value of the global `x` variable.

Functions in Python are a powerful feature that allow code to be organized, reused, and made more readable. By defining functions, programmers can break down complex tasks into smaller, manageable units, making the code easier to understand and maintain. Python provides a wide range of features for defining and using functions, including parameters, returns, default values, lambda functions, nesting, recursion, and scoping. By mastering functions in Python, programmers can write more efficient, modular, and flexible code.

7.Data structures: lists, tuples, dictionaries, sets in Python

Data structures are essential elements in programming that help organize and store data efficiently. In Python, a versatile and powerful programming language, there are various built-in data structures that can be used to manipulate and store data. Some of the commonly used data structures in Python include lists, tuples, dictionaries, and sets.

Lists in Python are ordered, mutable collections of elements that are indexed starting from 0. Lists can contain elements of different data types, including numbers, strings, and even other lists. Lists are created using square brackets [] and elements are separated by commas. Here is an example of a list in Python:

```python
```

```
my_list = [1, 2, 3, 'a', 'b', 'c']
```

Tuples are also ordered collections of elements, but unlike lists, tuples are immutable, meaning their elements cannot be changed once they are defined. Tuples are created using parentheses () and elements are separated by commas. Here is an example of a tuple in Python:

```python
my_tuple = (1, 2, 3, 'a', 'b', 'c')
```

Dictionaries are unordered collections of key-value pairs. Each key in a dictionary is unique and is associated with a value. Dictionaries are created using curly braces {} and key-value pairs are separated by colons (:). Here is an example of a dictionary in Python:

```python
my_dict = {'name': 'John', 'age': 30, 'city': 'New York'}
```

Sets in Python are unordered collections of unique elements. Sets do not allow duplicate elements and are used to perform mathematical set operations such as union, intersection, difference, etc. Sets are created using curly braces {} and elements are separated by commas. Here is an example of a set in Python:

```python
my_set = {1, 2, 3, 4, 5}
```

Each of these data structures has its own

characteristics and use cases, and understanding how to work with them is essential for every Python programmer.

Lists in Python are versatile and commonly used data structures that allow us to store and manipulate collections of elements. Lists are mutable, which means that their elements can be changed after they are created. Lists are ordered collections, which means that the order of elements in a list is fixed and can be accessed by index. Lists in Python are created using square brackets [] and elements are separated by commas. Here is an example of a list in Python:

```python
my_list = [1, 2, 3, 4, 5]
```

We can access elements in a list by their index. In Python, indexing starts from 0, which means that the first element in a list is at index 0, the second element is at index 1, and so on. We can also use negative indexing to access elements from the end of the list. We can access elements in a list using square brackets [] and the index of the element we want to access. Here are some examples:

```python
print(my_list[0])  # Output: 1
print(my_list[2])  # Output: 3
print(my_list[-1]) # Output: 5
```

We can also modify elements in a list by assigning new values to them. Lists are mutable, which means that we can change the elements of a list after it has been created. We can modify elements in a list by their index. Here is an example:

```python
my_list[2] = 10
print(my_list)  # Output: [1, 2, 10, 4, 5]
```

In addition to accessing and modifying elements, lists in Python support a variety of built-in methods for manipulating and working with lists. Some of the commonly used methods on lists include `append()`, `extend()`, `insert()`, `remove()`, `pop()`, `index()`, `reverse()`, and `sort()`. These methods can be used to add elements to a list, remove elements from a list, sort a list, and perform other operations on a list. Here are some examples:

```python
my_list.append(6)  # Append an element to the end of the list
my_list.extend([7, 8, 9])  # Extend the list
```

with another list

```
my_list.insert(3, 20)  # Insert an element at a specific index

my_list.remove(5)  # Remove a specific element from the list

my_list.pop()  # Remove and return the last element from the list

my_list.index(4)  # Find the index of a specific element in the list

my_list.reverse()  # Reverse the elements of the list

my_list.sort()  # Sort the elements of the list
```

Tuples in Python are similar to lists, but with one key difference - tuples are immutable. This means that once a tuple is created, its elements cannot be changed. Tuples are commonly used to represent fixed collections of elements, such as a coordinate pair or a date in a calendar. Tuples are created using parentheses () and elements are separated by commas. Here is an example of a tuple in Python:

```python
my_tuple = (1, 2, 3, 4, 5)
```

Tuples support similar indexing and slicing operations as lists, but because tuples are immutable, we cannot change the elements of a tuple after it has been created. Tuples can be useful in situations where we need to ensure that the elements of a collection are fixed and cannot be modified accidentally.

Dictionaries in Python are unordered collections of key-value pairs. Each key in a dictionary is unique and is associated with a value. Dictionaries are commonly used to represent mappings from keys to values, such as a phone book or a database of user information. Dictionaries are created using curly braces {} and key-value pairs are separated by colons (:). Here is an example of a dictionary in Python:

```python
my_dict = {'name': 'Alice', 'age': 25, 'city': 'Boston'}
```

We can access values in a dictionary by their keys. To retrieve the value associated with a key in a dictionary, we can use square brackets [] and the key of the element we want to access. Here is an example:

```python
print(my_dict['name'])  # Output: 'Alice'
print(my_dict['age'])   # Output: 25
```

We can also modify the values of keys in a dictionary by assigning new values to them. Dictionaries are mutable, which means that we can change the values of keys in a dictionary after it has been created. We can modify values in a dictionary by their keys. Here is an example:

```python
my_dict['age'] = 30
print(my_dict)  # Output: {'name': 'Alice', 'age': 30, 'city': 'Boston'}
```

In addition to accessing and modifying values, dictionaries in Python support a variety of built-in methods for manipulating and working with dictionaries. Some of the commonly used methods on dictionaries include `keys()`, `values()`, `items()`, `update()`, `pop()`, and `clear()`. These methods can be used to retrieve keys, values, or key-value pairs from a dictionary, add or remove key-value pairs, update the values of keys, and perform other operations on a dictionary. Here are some examples:

```python
print(my_dict.keys())  # Get a list of keys in the dictionary
print(my_dict.values())  # Get a list of values in the dictionary
print(my_dict.items())  # Get a list of key-value pairs in the dictionary
my_dict.update({'age': 35})  # Update the value of a key in the dictionary
my_dict.pop('city')  # Remove a key-value pair from the dictionary
my_dict.clear()  # Remove all key-value pairs from the dictionary
```

Sets in Python are unordered collections of unique elements. Sets are commonly used to perform mathematical set operations, such as union, intersection, difference, and symmetric difference. Sets do not allow duplicate elements and are used to store a collection of distinct values. Sets are created using curly braces {} and elements are separated by commas. Here is an example of a set in Python:

```python
my_set = {1, 2, 3, 4, 5}
```

Sets support a variety of set operations, such as union, intersection, difference, and symmetric difference. Sets in Python are mutable, which means that we can change the elements of a set after it has been created. We can modify elements in a set using methods such as `add()`, `update()`, `remove()`, `discard()`, `pop()`, and `clear()`. Here are some examples:

```python
my_set.add(6)  # Add an element to the set
my_set.update({7, 8, 9})  # Update the set with another set
my_set.remove(5)  # Remove a specific element from the set
my_set.discard(10)  # Remove a specific element from the set if it is present
my_set.pop()  # Remove and return an arbitrary element from the set
my_set.clear()  # Remove all elements from the set
```

In addition to these basic set operations, sets in Python support various mathematical set operations, such as union, intersection, difference, and symmetric difference. These operations can be performed using operators or methods on sets. Here are some examples:

```python
set1 = {1, 2, 3}
set2 = {3, 4, 5}

union_set = set1 | set2  # Union of two sets
intersection_set = set1 & set2  # Intersection of two sets
difference_set = set1 - set2  # Difference of two sets
symmetric_difference_set = set1 ^ set2  # Symmetric difference of two scts
```

Overall, lists, tuples, dictionaries, and sets are fundamental data structures in Python that are used to store, manipulate, and organize data efficiently. Each of these data structures has its own characteristics and use cases, and understanding how to work with them is essential for every Python programmer. By mastering these data structures, programmers can write more efficient and organized code, leading to better performance and easier maintenance of their programs.

8. Variables and Comments in Python

In Python, variables are used to store data values. These values can be numbers, strings, lists, dictionaries, or any other type of data that Python supports. Variables are created by assigning a value to a name, which can then be used to reference that value in code. Comments, on the other hand, are used to provide explanations or notes within the code that are not executed by the Python interpreter.

Variables in Python

In Python, variables are created by simply assigning a value to a name. The name of a variable can consist of letters, numbers, and underscores, but must start with a letter or an underscore. It is important to note that Python is a dynamically typed language, meaning that variables do not have a fixed type. This means that a variable can be reassigned to hold a different value of any type at any time.

Here is an example of creating and using variables in Python:

```python
x = 10
y = "Hello, World!"
z = [1, 2, 3]

print(x)
print(y)
print(z)
```

In this example, we have created three variables: x, y, and z. The variable "x" holds the integer value 10, the variable "y" holds the string value "Hello, World!", and the variable "z" holds a list of integers. We then use the print statement to display the values of these variables.

Comments in Python

Comments in Python are used to explain the purpose of the code or to provide additional information about the code. Comments are not executed by the Python interpreter and are ignored when the code is run. Comments can be single-line or multi-line, and are preceded by the "#" character.

Here is an example of single-line comments in Python:

```
# This is a single-line comment
```

And here is an example of multi-line comments in Python:

```
"""
This is a multi-line comment
that spans multiple lines
```

"""

Comments are useful for documenting code and making it easier for other programmers to understand. It is good practice to include comments in your code to explain the logic behind your implementation.

Examples of Variables and Comments in Python

Let's look at some examples that combine variables and comments in Python code:

Define variables

name = "Alice"

age = 30

height = 5.5

Print out the variables

```
print("Name:", name)

print("Age:", age)

print("Height:", height)
```

In this example, we have defined three variables: name, age, and height. We have assigned the values "Alice" to the name variable, 30 to the age variable, and 5.5 to the height variable. We then print out the values of these variables along with some additional information using comments.

```
# Calculate the sum of two numbers

num1 = 10

num2 = 20

sum = num1 + num2


# Print out the sum

print("The sum of", num1, "and", num2, "is", sum)
```

In this example, we have defined two variables num1 and num2, which hold the integer values 10 and 20 respectively. We then calculate the sum of these two numbers and store the result in the variable sum. Finally, we print out the sum along with some additional information using comments.

```python
# Define a list of names
names = ["Alice", "Bob", "Charlie"]

# Print out each name in the list
for name in names:
    print("Hello,", name)
```

In this example, we have defined a list variable called names, which contains three string values: Alice, Bob, and Charlie. We then loop through each name in the list and print out a greeting message for each name using comments.

Conclusion

Variables and comments are essential components of Python programming. Variables are used to store data values, while comments are used to provide explanations and notes within the code. By combining variables and comments effectively, you can write clear and well-documented code that is easy to understand and maintain.

By following best practices and using variables and comments appropriately, you can write clean and readable Python code that is easier to debug and modify. Remember to use descriptive variable names and informative comments to help other programmers (and your future self) understand your code more easily.

9.

Python is a versatile and popular programming language used by developers across the globe for various purposes. The key reason behind its popularity is the simplicity of its syntax and its readability.

In this article, we will explore the Python interpreter and the IDLE (Integrated Development and Learning Environment) in Python with examples to help you better understand how to use these powerful tools effectively in your programming journey.

The Python Interpreter:

The Python interpreter is a program that reads and executes Python code. It allows you to write and run Python code interactively, line by line, making it a great tool for testing your code before incorporating it into a larger program.

To access the Python interpreter, open your command prompt or terminal and type "python" to start the interactive Python shell. You will see a prompt that looks like ">>>", indicating that the interpreter is ready to accept your Python code.

You can then type Python code directly into the interpreter, and it will execute your code line by line, displaying the output immediately. For example, if you type "print('Hello, World!')" into the interpreter and press Enter, it will display "Hello, World!" as the output.

Here is an example of using the Python interpreter to execute a simple Python script:

```
```

```
>>> x = 5
>>> y = 10
>>> print(x + y)
15
```

In this example, we define two variables x and y, assign them values, and then print their sum. The interpreter executes the code line by line and displays the output after each line is executed.

The Python interpreter is an excellent tool for testing small snippets of code, debugging, and experimenting with Python features. However, for larger projects, you may want to use an IDE like IDLE.

IDLE (Integrated Development and Learning Environment) in Python:

IDLE is an integrated development environment that comes bundled with the standard Python distribution. It provides a more comprehensive set of tools for writing, editing, running, and debugging Python code compared to the basic Python interpreter.

To access IDLE, type "idle" into your command prompt or terminal and press Enter. This will open the IDLE editor, which consists of a Python shell window for interactive code execution and a code editor window for writing scripts.

The code editor in IDLE offers features like syntax highlighting, auto-completion, code folding, and more, making it easier to write and navigate through your Python code.

One of the primary advantages of using IDLE is that it allows you to save your Python scripts as .py files, making it easier to organize and run your code as standalone programs. You can also run your scripts from within IDLE by clicking the "Run" menu and selecting "Run Module" or by pressing F5.

Here is an example of writing and running a Python script in IDLE:

```python
# This is a simple Python script
x = 5
y = 10
print(x + y)
```

Save the above code as "simple_script.py" in IDLE, and then run the script by selecting "Run" > "Run Module" or by pressing F5. The output will be displayed in the Python shell window within IDLE.

In addition to writing and running Python scripts, IDLE also provides a debugging feature that allows you to set breakpoints, inspect variables, and trace the execution of your code. This can be incredibly useful for identifying and fixing errors in your programs.

In conclusion, the Python interpreter and IDLE are essential tools for Python programmers of all levels. The interpreter is great for quick testing and experimentation, while IDLE provides a more robust environment for writing, running, and debugging Python code.

By mastering these tools and practicing regularly, you can become proficient in Python programming and leverage its powerful features to develop a wide range of applications.

9.The Python interpreter and the IDLE in Python

Python is a versatile and popular programming language used by developers across the globe for various purposes. The key reason behind its popularity is the simplicity of its syntax and its readability.

In this article, we will explore the Python interpreter and the IDLE (Integrated Development and Learning Environment) in Python with examples to help you better understand how to use these powerful tools effectively in your programming journey.

The Python Interpreter:

The Python interpreter is a program that reads and executes Python code. It allows you to write and run Python code interactively, line by line, making it a great tool for testing your code before incorporating it into a larger program.

To access the Python interpreter, open your command prompt or terminal and type "python" to start the interactive Python shell. You will see a prompt that looks like ">>>", indicating that the interpreter is ready to accept your Python code.

You can then type Python code directly into the interpreter, and it will execute your code line by line, displaying the output immediately. For example, if you type "print('Hello, World!')" into the interpreter and press Enter, it will display "Hello, World!" as the output.

Here is an example of using the Python interpreter to execute a simple Python script:

```
```

```
>>> x = 5
>>> y = 10
>>> print(x + y)
15
```

In this example, we define two variables x and y, assign them values, and then print their sum. The interpreter executes the code line by line and displays the output after each line is executed.

The Python interpreter is an excellent tool for testing small snippets of code, debugging, and experimenting with Python features. However, for larger projects, you may want to use an IDE like IDLE.

IDLE (Integrated Development and Learning Environment) in Python:

IDLE is an integrated development environment that comes bundled with the standard Python distribution. It provides a more comprehensive set of tools for writing, editing, running, and debugging Python code compared to the basic Python interpreter.

To access IDLE, type "idle" into your command prompt or terminal and press Enter. This will open the IDLE editor, which consists of a Python shell window for interactive code execution and a code editor window for writing scripts.

The code editor in IDLE offers features like syntax highlighting, auto-completion, code folding, and more, making it easier to write and navigate through your Python code.

One of the primary advantages of using IDLE is that it allows you to save your Python scripts as .py files, making it easier to organize and run your code as standalone programs. You can also run your scripts from within IDLE by clicking the "Run" menu and selecting "Run Module" or by pressing F5.

Here is an example of writing and running a Python script in IDLE:

```python
# This is a simple Python script
x = 5
y = 10
print(x + y)
```

Save the above code as "simple_script.py" in IDLE, and then run the script by selecting "Run" > "Run Module" or by pressing F5. The output will be displayed in the Python shell window within IDLE.

In addition to writing and running Python scripts, IDLE also provides a debugging feature that allows you to set breakpoints, inspect variables, and trace the execution of your code. This can be incredibly useful for identifying and fixing errors in your programs.

In conclusion, the Python interpreter and IDLE are essential tools for Python programmers of all levels. The interpreter is great for quick testing and experimentation, while IDLE provides a more robust environment for writing, running, and debugging Python code.

By mastering these tools and practicing regularly, you can become proficient in Python programming and leverage its powerful features to develop a wide range of applications. Happy coding!

10. File handling in Python

File handling in Python is an essential skill that every programmer should have in their toolbox. It allows us to read and write data to and from files, which is crucial for working with larger datasets and storing information for future use. In this article, we will explore the basics of file handling in Python and learn how to perform common operations such as reading from and writing to files.

Reading from a file:

To read data from a file in Python, we need to first open the file using the built-in open() function. The open() function takes two arguments - the file path and the mode in which we want to open the file. The most common modes are 'r' for reading, 'w' for writing, and 'a' for appending.

Let's take a look at an example:

```python
# Open a file for reading
file = open('data.txt', 'r')

# Read the entire file
data = file.read()
print(data)

# Close the file
file.close()
```

In this example, we open a file called data.txt in read mode ('r'). We then use the read() method to read the entire contents of the file and store them in a variable called data. Finally, we close the file using the close()

method to free up system resources.

Writing to a file:

To write data to a file in Python, we again use the open() function but this time with the 'w' mode for writing. If the file does not exist, it will be created. If the file already exists, its contents will be overwritten. Let's see an example:

```python
# Open a file for writing
file = open('output.txt', 'w')

# Write some data to the file
file.write('Hello, World!\n')
file.write('This is a test\n')
```

```
# Close the file
file.close()
```

In this example, we open a file called output.txt in write mode ('w'). We then use the write() method to write two lines of text to the file. Each call to write() appends the given data to the file. Finally, we close the file to ensure that all changes are saved.

Appending to a file:

If we want to add new data to an existing file without overwriting its contents, we can use the 'a' mode for appending. Let's see an example:

```python
# Open a file for appending
```

```
file = open('output.txt', 'a')

# Append some data to the file
file.write('This is another line\n')
file.write('And one more for good measure\n')

# Close the file
file.close()
```

In this example, we open the file output.txt in append mode ('a'). We then use the write() method to add two new lines of text to the end of the file. The existing contents of the file remain untouched, and the new data is appended to the end.

Reading line by line:

When working with large files, reading the entire contents at once may not be practical. Instead, we can read the file line by line using a for loop. Let's see an example:

```python
# Open a file for reading
file = open('data.txt', 'r')

# Read the file line by line
for line in file:
    print(line)

# Close the file
file.close()
```

In this example, we open the file data.txt in read mode ('r'). We then iterate over the file object using a for loop, which reads the file line by line. Each iteration of the loop prints a line of text from the file.

Working with CSV files:

CSV (Comma Separated Values) files are commonly used to store tabular data, such as spreadsheets. Python provides a built-in csv module to make it easy to read and write CSV files. Let's see an example of reading from a CSV file:

```python
import csv

# Open a CSV file for reading
with open('data.csv', 'r') as file:
    reader = csv.reader(file)
    for row in reader:
```

    print(row)
```


In this example, we import the csv module, open a CSV file called data.csv in read mode, and create a csv.reader object to read the file. We then iterate over the rows in the file and print each row to the console.

Writing to a CSV file:

Similarly, we can write data to a CSV file using the csv.writer object. Let's see an example:

```python
import csv

# Open a CSV file for writing

```
with open('output.csv', 'w', newline='') as file:
    writer = csv.writer(file)
    writer.writerow(['Name', 'Age', 'City'])
    writer.writerow(['Alice', 30, 'New York'])
    writer.writerow(['Bob', 25, 'Los Angeles'])
```

In this example, we open a CSV file called output.csv in write mode and create a csv.writer object to write data to the file. We then use the writerow() method to write the column headers and two rows of data to the file.

Handling errors:

When working with files, it's important to handle errors that may occur during file operations, such as file not found or permission denied. We can use try-except blocks to catch and handle exceptions. Let's see an example:

```python
try:
    file = open('data.txt', 'r')
    data = file.read()
    print(data)
    file.close()
except FileNotFoundError:
    print('File not found')
except PermissionError:
    print('Permission denied')
```

In this example, we attempt to open a file called data.txt for reading and print its contents. If the file is not found, a FileNotFoundError exception is raised and caught by the except block. If a permission denied error occurs, a PermissionError exception is caught and handled accordingly.

Conclusion:

In this article, we have explored the basics of file handling in Python, including reading from and writing to files, appending data, working with CSV files, and handling errors. File handling is an important aspect of programming and is used in a wide range of applications, from data processing to web development. By mastering file handling in Python, you will be better equipped to work with files efficiently and effectively in your projects.

11. Working with modules and packages

Working with modules and packages in Python is an essential skill for any aspiring programmer. Modules and packages are a way to organize and structure your code, making it easier to manage and maintain. In this article, we will explore what modules and packages are, how to create and use them in your Python code, and why they are important.

First, let's start with modules. A module in Python is simply a file containing Python code. This code can define functions, classes, and variables that can be used in other Python files. Modules are a great way to organize your code and break it down into smaller, more manageable pieces. To create a module, you just need to create a new .py file and write your code inside it. For example, let's create a module called math_operations.py that contains some basic math functions:

```python
# math_operations.py

def add(x, y):
    return x + y

def subtract(x, y):
    return x - y

def multiply(x, y):
    return x * y

def divide(x, y):
    return x / y
```

Once you have created your module, you can

import it into another Python file using the import statement. For example, if you have a file called main.py and you want to use the functions defined in math_operations.py, you can do so like this:

```python
# main.py

import math_operations

result = math_operations.add(5, 3)
print(result)  # Output: 8

result = math_operations.multiply(4, 6)
print(result)  # Output: 24
```

In this example, we import the

math_operations module and use its add and multiply functions in our main.py file. This makes our code more organized and easier to understand.

But what if you have multiple modules that are related to each other? This is where packages come in. A package in Python is a way to organize multiple modules in a hierarchical directory structure. Packages allow you to group related modules together, making it easier to manage large codebases. To create a package, you simply need to create a directory with an __init__.py file inside it. For example, let's create a package called utils that contains the math_operations module:

```
utils/
    __init__.py
    math_operations.py
```

```

Inside the math_operations.py file, you can define your math functions as before. Then, in your main.py file, you can import the math_operations module from the utils package like this:

```python
# main.py

from utils import math_operations

result = math_operations.subtract(10, 5)
print(result)  # Output: 5
```

By using packages, you can organize your code in a way that reflects its logical structure.
```

This can make your codebase easier to navigate and maintain.

Another benefit of using modules and packages in Python is reusability. Once you have defined a module or package, you can import and use it in multiple Python files. This can save you time and effort, as you can avoid duplicating code across your projects. For example, if you have a set of utility functions that you use in multiple projects, you can create a utils package with those functions and import it whenever you need them.

In addition to making your code more organized and reusable, modules and packages in Python also help with namespacing. Namespacing is a way to prevent naming conflicts between different parts of your code. By organizing your code into modules and packages, you can avoid naming clashes and make your code more maintainable.

In summary, working with modules and packages in Python is a fundamental skill for any programmer. Modules are used to organize your code into smaller, more manageable pieces, while packages allow you to group related modules together in a hierarchical directory structure. By using modules and packages, you can make your code more organized, reusable, and maintainable. So next time you start a new Python project, consider using modules and packages to structure your code effectively.

12. Types of Data in Python with Examples

Python is a dynamically typed programming language, which means that the type of a variable is determined at runtime. There are several built-in data types in Python that represent various types of data, such as integers, strings, lists, tuples, dictionaries, and more. In this article, we will explore the different types of data in Python and provide examples of how they can be used.

1. Integers

Integers are whole numbers, positive or negative, without any decimal point. They can be written with or without a sign. In Python, integers are represented by the int class.

Example:

x = 5

y = -10

z = 0

2. Floats

Floats are numbers with a decimal point or numbers in scientific notation. In Python, floats are represented by the float class.

Example:

x = 3.14

y = -2.5

z = 1.23e6 # 1.23 x 10^6

3. Strings

Strings are sequences of characters, enclosed in single quotes, double quotes, or triple quotes. In Python, strings are immutable, which means they cannot be changed once they are created.

Example:

x = 'Hello, World!'

y = "Python is awesome"

z = '''This is a multiline

string in Python'''

4. Lists

Lists are ordered collections of items, which can be of any data type. In Python, lists are represented by the list class and can be modified by adding, removing, or changing elements.

Example:

x = [1, 2, 3, 4, 5]

y = ['apple', 'banana', 'cherry']

z = [1, 'a', True]

5. Tuples

Tuples are ordered collections of items, similar to lists, but they are immutable, which means they cannot be changed once they are created. In Python, tuples are represented by the tuple class.

Example:

x = (1, 2, 3)

y = ('apple', 'banana', 'cherry')

z = (1, 'a', True)

6. Dictionaries

Dictionaries are collections of key-value pairs, where each key is associated with a value. In Python, dictionaries are represented by the dict class and are mutable.

Example:

x = {'name': 'Alice', 'age': 30, 'city': 'New York'}

y = {1: 'apple', 2: 'banana', 3: 'cherry'}

z = {'a': 1, 'b': 2, 'c': 3}

7. Sets

Sets are unordered collections of unique elements. In Python, sets are represented by the set class and can be used to perform various set operations such as union, intersection, difference, and symmetric difference.

Example:

x = {1, 2, 3, 4, 5}

y = {'apple', 'banana', 'cherry'}

z = {1, 'a', True}

8. Booleans

Booleans are a data type that represents truth values, either True or False. In Python, booleans are represented by the bool class and are used in logical operations.

Example:

x = True

y = False

9. None

None is a special data type in Python that represents the absence of a value. It is often used to indicate that a variable has not been assigned a value.

Example:

x = None

10. Type Conversion

Python allows you to convert data from one type to another using built-in functions such as int(), float(), str(), list(), tuple(), dict(), set(), and bool().

Example:

x = 10

y = float(x)

z = str(x)

Python offers a variety of data types that allow you to work with different kinds of data efficiently. By understanding the various types of data in Python and how to use them, you can write more robust and flexible code for your projects.

13. The functions print and input and Indentation in Python

One of the key features of Python is its ease of use when it comes to printing output, taking user input, and using indentation for code readability. In this guide, we will explore the functions print() and input(), as well as the importance of proper indentation in Python programming.

1. The print() Function:

The print() function in Python is used to display output on the screen. It is a built-in function that takes one or more arguments and displays them as output. Here's a simple example of using the print() function:

```python
print("Hello, World!")
```

```

In this example, the print() function takes a single argument, the string "Hello, World!", and displays it on the screen. You can also pass multiple arguments to the print() function, separating them by commas:

```python
name = "Alice"
age = 30
print("My name is", name, "and I am", age, "years old.")
```

This code will output: "My name is Alice and I am 30 years old."

You can also use the print() function to display the values of variables, expressions,
```

and even the results of functions:

```python
x = 10
print("The value of x is:", x)

y = 5
z = x + y
print("The sum of x and y is:", z)
```

2. The input() Function:

The input() function in Python is used to take user input from the keyboard. It is a built-in function that displays a prompt to the user and waits for them to enter a value. Here's an example of using the input() function:

```python
name = input("Enter your name: ")
print("Hello, ", name)
```

When you run this code, the program will display the prompt "Enter your name: " and wait for the user to enter their name. Once the user enters their name and presses enter, the program will display "Hello, " followed by the entered name.

You can also use the input() function to take numerical input from the user:

```python
age = int(input("Enter your age: "))
print("You are", age, "years old.")
```

In this example, the input() function takes the user's input as a string, so we use the int() function to convert it to an integer before printing the output.

3. Indentation in Python:

In Python, indentation is used to define the structure of the code. Instead of using braces {} or begin/end keywords like other programming languages, Python uses indentation to indicate where blocks of code begin and end. Proper indentation is crucial for the readability and functionality of Python code. Here's an example of indentation in Python:

```python
if x > 0:
    print("x is positive.")
```

```
else:
    print("x is non-positive.")
```

In this code snippet, the if statement block is indented by four spaces, and the else block is also indented by four spaces. The indentation levels define the scope of each block of code. Improper indentation will result in syntax errors, so it's essential to pay attention to the correct indentation in Python.

You can also use indentation in loops, functions, classes, and other structures in Python:

```python
def greet():
    print("Hello!")
    print("Welcome to Python programming.")
```

greet()

```
```

In this example, the function greet() is defined with proper indentation, and the statements inside the function are also indented. When the function is called using greet(), the indented statements will be executed as part of the function's block.

The print() and input() functions are essential for displaying output and taking user input in Python. Indentation is a crucial aspect of Python programming that defines the structure and readability of the code. By understanding and using these features effectively, you can write clear and concise Python code for a wide range of applications.

14. Numbers and logical operators in Python strings

In Python, there are several built-in data types that we can use to represent different kinds of information. One of the most common data types is the string, which is used to represent a sequence of characters. Strings in Python are enclosed in either single quotes (') or double quotes (""). For example:

```
name = 'Alice'
```

Strings can be concatenated using the `+` operator:

```
greeting = 'Hello, ' + name
print(greeting)  # Output: Hello, Alice
```

```

Strings can also be repeated using the `*` operator:

```

repeated_greeting = greeting * 3

print(repeated_greeting) # Output: Hello, AliceHello, AliceHello, Alice

```

We can access individual characters in a string using square brackets `[ ]`:

```

print(name[0]) # Output: A

```

In Python, strings are zero-indexed, meaning that the first character of a string has an index of 0, the second character has an index of 1,
```

and so on.

We can also use slicing to extract a substring from a string. Slicing is done by specifying a range of indices enclosed in square brackets `[start:end]`. The `start` index is inclusive, while the `end` index is exclusive. For example:

```
print(name[0:2])  # Output: Al
```

If we omit the `start` or `end` index, Python assumes it to be the beginning or end of the string, respectively:

```
print(name[:2])   # Output: Al
print(name[2:])   # Output: ice
```

Strings in Python are immutable, meaning that once a string is created, its contents cannot be changed. However, we can create a new string that is a modification of the original string:

```
new_name = name.replace('A', 'B')

print(new_name)  # Output: Blice
```

Python also provides numerous built-in string methods for manipulating strings. Some common string methods include `upper()`, `lower()`, `strip()`, `find()`, `replace()`, `split()`, and `join()`. For example:

```
sentence = ' Hello, World! '

print(sentence.strip())  # Output: 'Hello, World!'

print(sentence.find('World'))  # Output: 9

print(sentence.split(', '))  # Output: [' Hello',
```

'World! ']

```

In addition to string manipulation, Python also allows us to work with numbers and logical operators.

Numerical data types in Python include integers, floating-point numbers, and complex numbers. We can perform basic arithmetic operations such as addition (+), subtraction (-), multiplication (*), division (/), and exponentiation (**):

```
x = 5
y = 2

print(x + y) # Output: 7
print(x - y) # Output: 3
print(x * y) # Output: 10

```
print(x / y)  # Output: 2.5
print(x ** y) # Output: 25
```

Python also provides functions for rounding, absolute value, and type conversion:

```
print(round(3.14159, 2))  # Output: 3.14
print(abs(-10))           # Output: 10
print(int(3.14))          # Output: 3
print(float(3))           # Output: 3.0
```

Logical operators in Python include `and`, `or`, and `not`. These operators are used to combine or negate logical values True and False. For example:

```
a = True
```

```
b = False

print(a and b)  # Output: False
print(a or b)   # Output: True
print(not a)    # Output: False
```

We can also use comparison operators to compare values and produce a Boolean result. Comparison operators include `==` (equal to), `!=` (not equal to), `<` (less than), `>` (greater than), `<=` (less than or equal to), and `>=` (greater than or equal to). For example:

```
print(5 == 5)   # Output: True
print(5 != 5)   # Output: False
print(5 < 10)   # Output: True
print(5 >= 5)   # Output: True
```

Conditional statements in Python use logical operators and comparison operators to control the flow of the program. We can use `if`, `elif`, and `else` statements to execute different blocks of code based on certain conditions. For example:

```
x = 10

if x > 5:
    print('x is greater than 5')
elif x < 5:
    print('x is less than 5')
else:
    print('x is equal to 5')
```

We can also use nested conditional statements

and logical operators to create more complex conditions:

```
grade = 75

if grade >= 90:
    print('A')
elif grade >= 80 and grade < 90:
    print('B')
elif grade >= 70 and grade < 80:
    print('C')
else:
    print('F')
```

In conclusion, Python provides powerful features for working with strings, numbers, and logical operators. By understanding and mastering these concepts, you can write more sophisticated and versatile programs in Python. Whether you are manipulating text, performing numerical calculations, or making decisions based on logical conditions, Python's built-in functions and operators make it easy to work with a wide range of data types and operations.

15. Dictionary

In Python, a dictionary is a collection of key-value pairs, where each key is associated with a value. Dictionaries are mutable, unordered collections of items, and they can be created using curly braces {} with key-value pairs separated by colons :. Dictionaries are useful for storing and retrieving data based on keys rather than numerical indexes.

Dictionaries can store any data type as a value, including strings. This makes dictionaries a powerful tool for organizing and manipulating data in Python. When working with strings, dictionaries can be used to store and retrieve information based on keys that are related to the string data.

Here's an example of how dictionaries can be used with strings in Python:

```python
# Creating a dictionary to store information about a person

person = {

    "name": "John Doe",

    "age": 30,

    "occupation": "Software Developer",

    "location": "New York"

}


# Accessing values in the dictionary using keys

print(person["name"])  # Output: John Doe

print(person["occupation"])  # Output: Software Developer


# Adding a new key-value pair to the dictionary

person["email"] = "johndoe@example.com"
```

```python
# Modifying the value of an existing key
person["age"] = 31


# Removing a key-value pair from the dictionary
del person["location"]


# Iterating over the keys and values in the dictionary
for key, value in person.items():
    print(f"{key}: {value}")


# Output:
# name: John Doe
# age: 31
# occupation: Software Developer
# email: johndoe@example.com
```

```

In the example above, we created a dictionary called `person` that stores information about a person. We accessed values in the dictionary using keys, added a new key-value pair, modified the value of an existing key, removed a key-value pair, and iterated over the keys and values in the dictionary.

Dictionaries are also commonly used to count the occurrences of characters or words in a string. This can be done by iterating over the characters in the string and updating the counts in the dictionary. Here's an example of how this can be achieved:

```python
# Counting the occurrences of characters in a string
s = "hello world"

```python
char_counts = {}

for char in s:
    if char in char_counts:
        char_counts[char] += 1
    else:
        char_counts[char] = 1

# Displaying the character counts
for char, count in char_counts.items():
    print(f"{char}: {count}")

# Output:
# h: 1
# e: 1
# l: 3
# o: 2
```

```
# : 1

# w: 1

# r: 1

# d: 1
```

In the example above, we created a dictionary called `char_counts` to store the occurrences of characters in the string `s`. We iterated over each character in the string, checked if the character was already in the dictionary, and updated the count accordingly. Finally, we displayed the character counts by iterating over the dictionary.

Dictionaries can also be used with strings to create lookup tables for mapping values to other values. For example, you can create a dictionary that maps abbreviations to their full forms, or vice versa. Here's an example of how this can be implemented:

```python
# Creating a dictionary to map abbreviations to full forms
abbreviations = {
    "CA": "California",
    "NY": "New York",
    "TX": "Texas"
}


# Using the dictionary to retrieve full forms based on abbreviations
print(abbreviations["CA"])  # Output: California
print(abbreviations["NY"])  # Output: New York


# Adding a new abbreviation to the dictionary
abbreviations["FL"] = "Florida"
```

```python
# Modifying the full form of an existing abbreviation
abbreviations["TX"] = "Taxes"

# Removing an abbreviation from the dictionary
del abbreviations["NY"]

# Iterating over the abbreviations and full forms in the dictionary
for abbreviation, full_form in abbreviations.items():
    print(f"{abbreviation}: {full_form}")

# Output:
# CA: California
# TX: Taxes
# FL: Florida
```

```

In the example above, we created a dictionary called `abbreviations` to map abbreviations to their full forms. We used the dictionary to retrieve full forms based on abbreviations, added a new abbreviation, modified the full form of an existing abbreviation, removed an abbreviation, and iterated over the abbreviations and full forms in the dictionary.

Dictionaries in Python are versatile data structures that can be used effectively with strings to store, retrieve, manipulate, and organize data based on keys. By combining dictionaries with strings, you can create powerful tools for handling text data in Python.
```

16. Set and frozenset are built-in types

In Python, the set and frozenset are two built-in data types that represent collections of unique elements. Sets are mutable, unordered collections of unique elements, while frozensets are immutable sets. Both sets and frozensets can contain any hashable data type, such as integers, strings, tuples, and other sets.

Sets are created using curly braces {} or the set() constructor. Frozensets are created using the frozenset() constructor. Let's take a closer look at these two data types with some examples:

1. Set:

a. Creating a set:

```python
my_set = {1, 2, 3, 4, 5}
```

```python
print(my_set)  # Output: {1, 2, 3, 4, 5}
```

b. Adding elements to a set:

```python
my_set.add(6)
print(my_set)  # Output: {1, 2, 3, 4, 5, 6}
```

c. Removing elements from a set:

```python
my_set.remove(2)
print(my_set)  # Output: {1, 3, 4, 5, 6}
```

d. Set operations:

```python
```

```python
set1 = {1, 2, 3}
set2 = {3, 4, 5}

# Union
print(set1 | set2)  # Output: {1, 2, 3, 4, 5}

# Intersection
print(set1 & set2)  # Output: {3}

# Difference
print(set1 - set2)  # Output: {1, 2}
```

2. Frozenset:

a. Creating a frozenset:
```python
```

```python
my_frozenset = frozenset([1, 2, 3, 4, 5])
print(my_frozenset)  # Output: frozenset({1, 2, 3, 4, 5})
```

b. Frozensets are immutable:

```python
my_frozenset.add(6)  # This will raise an AttributeError
```

c. Frozenset operations:

```python
frozenset1 = frozenset({1, 2, 3})
frozenset2 = frozenset({3, 4, 5})

# Union
print(frozenset1 | frozenset2)  # Output:
```

```
frozenset({1, 2, 3, 4, 5})


# Intersection
print(frozenset1 & frozenset2)  # Output: frozenset({3})


# Difference
print(frozenset1 - frozenset2)  # Output: frozenset({1, 2})
```

Sets and frozensets are particularly useful when you need to work with collections of unique elements and perform set operations like union, intersection, and difference. Sets are more commonly used due to their mutability, while frozensets are used in scenarios where immutability is desired. Both data types provide efficient ways to handle collections of unique elements in Python.

17. Conditional Statements, Loops: for and while in Python

Python is a versatile programming language that provides developers with a wide range of tools to efficiently manage and process data. Among the most important features of Python are conditional statements and loops, which allow for the execution of specific blocks of code based on certain conditions, or repeatedly based on predefined conditions. In this guide, we will delve into conditional statements and two types of loops in Python: the for loop and the while loop.

Conditional Statements:

Conditional statements are used to perform different actions based on different conditions. The most commonly used conditional statements in Python are if, elif, and else.

1. If Statement:

The if statement is used to execute a block of code only if a certain condition is true. The syntax of the if statement is as follows:

if condition:

   statement(s)

For example, consider the following code snippet:

x = 10

if x > 5:

   print("x is greater than 5")

In this example, the print statement will only be executed if the condition x > 5 is true.

2. Else Statement:

The else statement is used to execute a block

of code if the condition specified in the if statement is false. The syntax of the else statement is as follows:

if condition:

    statement(s)

else:

    statement(s)

Continuing with the previous example:

x = 3

if x > 5:

    print("x is greater than 5")

else:

    print("x is less than or equal to 5")

In this case, since x is less than 5, the else

statement will be executed.

3. Elif Statement:

The elif statement is used to check additional conditions if the preceding condition(s) are false. The syntax of an if...elif...else statement is as follows:

if condition1:

   statement(s)

elif condition2:

   statement(s)

else:

   statement(s)

Consider the following example:

x = 5

```python
if x > 5:
    print("x is greater than 5")
elif x == 5:
    print("x is equal to 5")
else:
    print("x is less than 5")
```

In this case, the elif statement checks if x is equal to 5 after the first condition is false.

Loops:

Loops in Python are used to repeat a specific block of code for a certain number of times or until a certain condition is met. Python provides two main types of loops: the for loop and the while loop.

1. For Loop:

The for loop is used to iterate over a sequence

of elements, such as lists, tuples, or strings. The syntax of the for loop is as follows:

for item in sequence:

   statement(s)

Consider the following example:

fruits = ["apple", "banana", "cherry"]

for fruit in fruits:

   print(fruit)

In this example, the for loop iterates over each item in the fruits list and prints it.

2. While Loop:

The while loop is used to execute a block of code as long as a specified condition is true. The syntax of the while loop is as follows:

```
while condition:
    statement(s)
```

The following example prints numbers from 1 to 5 using a while loop:

```
i = 1
while i <= 5:
    print(i)
    i += 1
```

In this case, the while loop will continue to execute as long as the condition i <= 5 is true.

Combining Conditional Statements and Loops:

Conditional statements and loops can be combined to create more complex programs that can perform a variety of tasks. Consider the following example, which uses a for loop and conditions to check whether a number is prime:

```
num = 13
is_prime = True

if num < 2:
    is_prime = False
else:
    for i in range(2, num):
        if num % i == 0:
            is_prime = False
            break

if is_prime:
    print(num, "is a prime number")
```

else:

   print(num, "is not a prime number")

In this example, the program checks whether the number 13 is prime by iterating through all numbers from 2 up to num-1 and checking if num is divisible by any of them. If the program finds a divisor, it sets the is_prime flag to False, indicating that the number is not prime.

Conditional statements and loops are essential programming concepts that are frequently used in Python to control the flow of execution and iterate through data. By understanding how to use if...elif...else statements, for loops, and while loops, developers can create powerful and efficient programs that can perform a wide range of tasks. Experimenting with these concepts and practicing writing code using conditional statements and loops will help you build your skills as a Python programmer.

18. Functions and directives in Python

Python is a versatile and powerful programming language that offers many built-in functions and methods to perform various operations. These functions and methods help in simplifying the code and making it more readable and efficient. In this article, we will explore some of the commonly used functions and directives in Python along with examples.

1. Built-in Functions:

Python provides a wide range of built-in functions that can be used to perform different tasks. Some of the commonly used built-in functions are:

a. print(): The print() function is used to display output on the console. For example:

```python
```

```
print("Hello, World!")
```

b. len(): The len() function returns the length of a string, list, tuple, dictionary, etc. For example:

```python
str = "Python"
print(len(str))
```

c. range(): The range() function generates a sequence of numbers within a specified range. For example:

```python
for i in range(5):
    print(i)
```

d. type(): The type() function returns the data type of an object. For example:

```python
num = 10
print(type(num))
```

e. sum(): The sum() function returns the sum of all elements in a list. For example:

```python
list = [1, 2, 3, 4, 5]
print(sum(list))
```

2. User-defined Functions:

In addition to built-in functions, Python allows us to define our custom functions that can perform specific tasks. We can define a function using the def keyword followed by the function name and parameters. Here is an example of a user-defined function that calculates the square of a number:

```python
def square(num):
    return num ** 2

result = square(5)
print(result)
```

3. Lambda Functions:

Lambda functions are anonymous functions that can have any number of arguments but only one expression. These functions are defined using the lambda keyword. Lambda functions are often used when a small function is required for a short period. Here is an example of a lambda function that calculates the cube of a number:

```python
cube = lambda x: x ** 3

result = cube(4)

print(result)
```

4. Map and Filter Functions:

The map() function in Python applies a function to each item in an iterable (such as a list) and returns an iterator with the results. The syntax of the map() function is map(function, iterable). Here is an example of using the map() function to calculate the square of each element in a list:

```python
numbers = [1, 2, 3, 4, 5]

squared = map(lambda x: x ** 2, numbers)
```

```
print(list(squared))
```

The filter() function in Python creates a new list that contains only elements that satisfy a certain condition. The syntax of the filter() function is filter(function, iterable). Here is an example of using the filter() function to filter out odd numbers from a list:

```python
numbers = [1, 2, 3, 4, 5]
odd_numbers = filter(lambda x: x % 2 != 0, numbers)
print(list(odd_numbers))
```

5. List Comprehensions:

List comprehensions provide a concise way to create lists in Python. They allow us to build lists by applying an expression to each item in an iterable. Here is an example of a list comprehension that generates a list containing the square of numbers from 1 to 5:

```python
squared = [x ** 2 for x in range(1, 6)]
print(squared)
```

6. Error Handling:

Python provides a way to handle errors using try...except blocks. This allows us to catch exceptions and handle them gracefully. Here is an example of using try...except blocks to handle a ZeroDivisionError:

```python
try:
    result = 10 / 0
except ZeroDivisionError:
```

```
    print("Division by zero is not allowed")
```

7. Docstrings:

Docstrings are used to provide documentation for functions, modules, classes, or methods in Python. They are enclosed in triple quotes and are the first statement in the body of the function or class. Docstrings help in understanding the purpose of the code and how to use it. Here is an example of a function with a docstring:

```python
def say_hello(name):
    """
    This function greets the user with the provided name.
    """
    print("Hello, " + name)
```

```python
say_hello("Alice")
```

8. Decorators:

Decorators are a powerful tool in Python that allows you to modify or extend the behavior of functions or methods without changing their code. Decorators are functions themselves that take another function as an argument and return a new function. Here is an example of a decorator that prints a message before and after executing a function:

```python
def decorator(func):
    def wrapper():
        print("Before executing the function")
        func()
        print("After executing the function")
```

```
    return wrapper

@decorator
def greet():
    print("Hello!")

greet()
```

9. Global and Local Variables:

Python allows you to define variables at different scopes. Global variables are defined outside any function or class and can be accessed anywhere in the program. Local variables are defined within a function or method and are only accessible within that function or method. Here is an example that demonstrates the difference between global and local variables:

```python
global_var = "I am a global variable"

def function():
    local_var = "I am a local variable"
    print(global_var)
    print(local_var)

function()
print(global_var)
# print(local_var) # This will raise an error as local_var is not accessible outside the function
```

Python offers a wide range of built-in functions, user-defined functions, lambda functions, map and filter functions, list comprehensions, error handling, docstrings, decorators, and variable scopes to make coding easier and more efficient. By mastering these functions and directives, you can write clean, readable, and maintainable code in Python.

19. Error handling and exceptions in Python

Error handling is an essential aspect of programming in Python (and in any other programming language), as it allows developers to anticipate and deal with unexpected issues that may arise during the execution of a program. Python provides a number of tools and constructs that can be used to handle errors and exceptions effectively.

Exceptions in Python

In Python, exceptions are special objects that are raised when an error occurs during the execution of a program. When an exception is raised, the program stops executing normally and jumps to the closest exception handler to deal with the error. Exceptions can be raised explicitly using the `raise` statement, or they can be raised implicitly by the interpreter when an error occurs. Some common built-in exceptions in Python include `TypeError`, `ValueError`, `ZeroDivisionError`, and `ImportError`.

try-except block

One of the most common ways to handle exceptions in Python is by using the try-except block. The try-except block allows developers to catch exceptions that are raised within a block of code and handle them gracefully. Here is a simple example of a try-except block in Python:

```
try:
    x = 10 / 0
except ZeroDivisionError:
    print("Division by zero!")
```

In this example, the division by zero error is anticipated, and the program will print "Division by zero!" instead of crashing when the error occurs. The `except` clause specifies the type of exception that should be caught, and the block of code inside this clause is executed when that exception is raised.

Multiple except blocks

Python allows developers to handle multiple types of exceptions using separate `except` blocks. This can be useful when different types of errors need to be handled differently. Here is an example that demonstrates the use of multiple `except` blocks:

```
try:
    file = open("nonexistent_file.txt", "r")
    content = file.read()
    file.close()
```

```
except FileNotFoundError:
    print("File not found!")
except IOError:
    print("An error occurred while reading the file!")
```

In this example, the program tries to open a nonexistent file for reading, and the appropriate error message is printed based on the type of exception that is raised.

else and finally blocks

In addition to the `try` and `except` blocks, Python also provides the `else` and `finally` blocks that can be used to further customize error handling. The `else` block is executed only if no exceptions are raised in the try block, while the `finally` block is always executed, whether an exception is raised or not. Here is an example that uses both `else` and `finally` blocks:

```
try:
    x = 10 / 2
except ZeroDivisionError:
    print("Division by zero!")
else:
    print("Division successful!")
finally:
    print("Finally block executed!")
```

In this example, since the division operation is successful, the "Division successful!" message is printed in the `else` block, and the "Finally block executed!" message is printed in the `finally` block.

Custom exceptions

In addition to built-in exceptions, Python allows developers to define custom exceptions by subclassing the built-in `Exception` class. This can be useful when specific types of errors need to be handled in a unique way. Here is an example of creating and raising a custom exception in Python:

```
class CustomError(Exception):
    def __init__(self, message):
        self.message = message

    def __str__(self):
        return f'CustomError: {self.message}'

try:
    raise CustomError("This is a custom error message.")
```

```
except CustomError as e:
    print(e)
```

In this example, a custom exception `CustomError` is defined with a custom error message. The exception is raised inside a try block and caught in the except block, where the custom error message is printed.

Handling exceptions in functions

It is also important to consider error handling when defining functions in Python. When a function raises an exception, it can be caught and handled in the calling code. Here is an example that demonstrates error handling in a function:

```
def divide(x, y):
```

```
try:
    result = x / y
except ZeroDivisionError:
    print("Division by zero!")
else:
    return result

print(divide(10, 2))
print(divide(10, 0))
```

In this example, the `divide` function performs a division operation, and any division by zero errors are caught and handled inside the function. The calling code prints the result of the division operation for valid inputs and prints an error message for invalid inputs.

Error handling is a crucial aspect of writing robust and reliable code in Python. By using the various tools and constructs provided by the language, developers can anticipate and handle errors and exceptions gracefully, leading to more resilient and maintainable software. From the try-except block to custom exceptions, Python offers a wide range of features that make error handling a straightforward and manageable task for developers.

20. Object-oriented programming in Python Working with classes and objects

Object-oriented programming (OOP) is a programming paradigm that uses "objects" – data structures consisting of data fields and methods – to design applications and computer programs. Python is a popular high-level programming language that fully supports object-oriented programming.

In Python, everything is an object, and you can easily create your objects and classes. Let's dive into the basics of working with classes and objects in Python.

Classes in Python

A class is like a blueprint for creating objects in Python. It defines the attributes (data fields) and behaviors (methods) that each instance of the class will have. To define a class in Python, you use the `class` keyword followed by the class name. Here's an example of a simple `Person` class:

```python
class Person:
    def __init__(self, name, age):
        self.name = name
        self.age = age

    def greet(self):
        return f"Hello, my name is {self.name} and I am {self.age} years old."
```

In this example, we have defined a `Person` class with two attributes: `name` and `age`, and one method:` greet`. The `__init__` method is a special method in Python called a constructor, which is called when a new instance of the class is created.

Objects in Python

Once we have defined a class, we can create objects (instances) of that class. To create an object, you simply call the class name as if it were a function, with any required arguments. For example:

```python
person1 = Person("Alice", 30)
person2 = Person("Bob", 25)
```

In this code snippet, we have created two instances of the `Person` class: `person1` and `person2`. Each object has its copy of the attributes `name` and `age`.

Accessing Attributes and Methods

Once we have created objects, we can access

their attributes and methods using the dot notation. For example:

```python
print(person1.name)  # Output: Alice
print(person2.age)  # Output: 25


print(person1.greet())  # Output: Hello, my name is Alice and I am 30 years old.
print(person2.greet())  # Output: Hello, my name is Bob and I am 25 years old.
```

In the above code, we are printing the attributes `name` and `age` of `person1` and `person2`, as well as calling the `greet` method on each object.

Inheritance in Python

Another important feature of object-oriented programming is inheritance. Inheritance allows you to create a new class based on an existing class, where the new class inherits the attributes and methods of the parent class. In Python, you define inheritance by putting the parent class in parentheses after the new class name. Here's an example:

```python
class Student(Person):
    def __init__(self, name, age, student_id):
        super().__init__(name, age)
        self.student_id = student_id

    def study(self, subject):
        return f"{self.name} is studying {subject}."
```

In this example, we have created a `Student` class that inherits from the `Person` class. The `Student` class has an additional attribute `student_id` and a method `study`.

Polymorphism in Python

Polymorphism is the ability for objects of different classes to respond to the same method in different ways. This makes code more flexible and allows for cleaner and more concise code. In Python, polymorphism is implemented through method overriding, where a subclass provides a specific implementation of a method that is already defined in the superclass. Here's an example:

```python
class Dog:
    def speak(self):
        return "Woof!"
```

```python
class Cat:
    def speak(self):
        return "Meow!"

def pet_speak(pet):
    return pet.speak()

dog = Dog()
cat = Cat()

print(pet_speak(dog))  # Output: Woof!
print(pet_speak(cat))  # Output: Meow!
```

In this example, both the `Dog` and `Cat` classes have a `speak` method. By passing an object of either class to the `pet_speak` function, we can see how polymorphism allows objects of different classes to respond differently to the same method call.

Encapsulation in Python

Encapsulation is the concept of restricting access to certain parts of an object and exposing only what is necessary. In Python, you can achieve encapsulation by using private attributes and methods. Private attributes and methods are denoted by a double underscore `__` prefix. Here's an example:

```python
class BankAccount:
    def __init__(self, balance):
        self.__balance = balance

    def deposit(self, amount):
        self.__balance += amount
```

```
    def withdraw(self, amount):
        if amount <= self.__balance:
            self.__balance -= amount
        else:
            print("Insufficient funds.")

    def get_balance(self):
        return self.__balance
```

In this example, the `balance` attribute is private and cannot be accessed directly from outside the class. Instead, you can only modify it using the `deposit` and `withdraw` methods. The `get_balance` method allows for read-only access to the `balance` attribute.

Object-oriented programming in Python provides a powerful way to organize and structure your code by defining classes and objects. Classes act as blueprints for creating objects, and inheritance allows you to build upon existing classes to create new ones. Polymorphism enables flexibility in how objects respond to method calls, while encapsulation helps restrict access to certain parts of an object.

By understanding and utilizing these concepts, you can write more maintainable, reusable, and scalable code in Python. Experiment with creating your classes and objects, and explore how OOP can benefit your programming projects.

21. Exception Handling and File Handling in Python: Managing Modules and Creating New Modules

In Python, exception handling is a crucial aspect of writing robust and reliable code. When a program encounters an error, exceptions are raised, and if not handled properly, they can lead to crashes and unexpected behavior. By using try-except blocks, developers can catch and handle exceptions gracefully, allowing the program to continue running without disruptions.

File handling is another essential feature in Python, enabling developers to read, write, and manipulate files on the system. By using various file handling functions and methods, programmers can interact with files, such as reading data from a file, writing data to a file, or modifying existing files.

In this article, we will explore how to manage

exceptions and handle files in Python, with a focus on creating and using modules in our code. We will cover the basics of exception handling, file management, and modular programming in Python, along with examples to demonstrate these concepts in action.

Exception Handling in Python:

Exception handling in Python allows developers to anticipate and handle errors that may occur during the execution of a program. By using try-except blocks, programmers can catch exceptions and handle them appropriately, preventing crashes and maintaining the program's stability. Here is a basic example of exception handling in Python:

```python
try:
    result = 10 / 0
```

```
    except ZeroDivisionError:
        print("Division by zero is not allowed")
```

In this code snippet, the try block attempts to divide 10 by 0, which will raise a ZeroDivisionError. The except block catches this exception and prints a custom error message, preventing the program from crashing.

Python provides a range of built-in exception classes to handle different types of errors, such as ZeroDivisionError, ValueError, TypeError, and more. Developers can also create custom exception classes by inheriting from the Exception class and defining their specific error conditions.

File Handling in Python:

File handling in Python allows developers to interact with files on the system, performing operations such as reading data from files, writing data to files, and managing file objects. Python provides built-in functions and methods for file handling, making it easy to work with files in various formats.

Here is an example of reading data from a file in Python:

```python
# Open a file in read mode
file = open("example.txt", "r")

# Read the contents of the file
data = file.read()

# Close the file
file.close()
```

print(data)

```

In this code snippet, we open a file named "example.txt" in read mode, read the contents of the file using the read() method, and then close the file using the close() method. It's essential to close the file after reading or writing to avoid memory leaks and ensure proper file handling.

Creating Modules in Python:

Modules in Python are reusable pieces of code that can be imported into other programs to provide additional functionality. By organizing code into modules, developers can promote code reusability, maintainability, and readability in their projects. Python modules are stored in separate .py files, which contain functions, classes, and variables that can be
```

imported and used in other Python scripts.

Here is an example of creating a simple Python module named "math_operations.py":

math_operations.py:

```python
def add(a, b):
    return a + b

def subtract(a, b):
    return a - b

def multiply(a, b):
    return a * b

def divide(a, b):
```

```python
    try:
        return a / b
    except ZeroDivisionError:
        return "Division by zero is not allowed"
```

In this module, we define four math operation functions: add, subtract, multiply, and divide. These functions can be imported into other Python scripts by using the import statement:

```python
import math_operations

result = math_operations.add(5, 3)
print(result)
```

By importing the math_operations module, we can access and use its functions in our main program. This modular approach to programming encourages code organization, reusability, and maintainability, making it easier to manage large codebases and collaborate with other developers.

In this article, we have discussed exception handling, file handling, and module creation in Python. Exception handling allows developers to catch and handle errors gracefully, preventing crashes and maintaining the program's stability. File handling enables programmers to read, write, and manipulate files on the system, facilitating data input/output operations. Module creation promotes code reusability, maintainability, and readability by encapsulating functionality into reusable components.

By mastering these concepts and techniques in

Python, developers can write more robust, reliable, and maintainable code, leading to improved productivity and efficiency in their software development projects. By understanding how to manage exceptions, handle files, and create modules effectively, programmers can enhance the quality and performance of their Python programs, ultimately delivering better solutions to users and clients alike.

22. Special Methods in Python: Unlocking the Power of Object-Oriented Programming

Introduction:

One of the key features of Python is its support for object-oriented programming (OOP) which allows programmers to create classes and objects to model real-world entities. Special methods in Python are a set of predefined methods that begin and end with double underscores (__). These methods are also known as magic methods or dunder methods and provide a way to customize the behavior of objects in Python.

In this article, we will explore some of the most commonly used special methods in Python and demonstrate how they can be used to take advantage of the power of object-oriented programming.

1. `__init__` Method:

The `__init__` method is a special method used to initialize objects of a class. When a new object is created, this method is automatically called to initialize its attributes. Let's take a look at an example:

```python
class Person:
    def __init__(self, name, age):
        self.name = name
        self.age = age

    def __str__(self):
        return f"Person(name={self.name}, age={self.age})"
```

```python
person = Person("Alice", 30)
print(person)  # Output: Person(name=Alice, age=30)
```

In this example, the `__init__` method is used to initialize the `name` and `age` attributes of the `Person` class. The `__str__` method is also defined to customize the string representation of the `Person` object.

2. `__repr__` Method:

The `__repr__` method is a special method used to return a string representation of an object. This method is called by the `repr` built-in function if present. Let's see an example:

```python
```

```python
class Point:
    def __init__(self, x, y):
        self.x = x
        self.y = y

    def __repr__(self):
        return f"Point(x={self.x}, y={self.y})"

point = Point(5, 10)
print(repr(point))  # Output: Point(x=5, y=10)
```

In this example, the `__repr__` method is defined to return a string representation of the `Point` object. When `repr(point)` is called, the `__repr__` method is invoked.

3. `__add__` Method:

The `__add__` method is a special method used to define the behavior of the `+` operator for objects of a class. Let's look at an example:

```python
class Vector:
    def __init__(self, x, y):
        self.x = x
        self.y = y

    def __add__(self, other):
        return Vector(self.x + other.x, self.y + other.y)

    def __str__(self):
        return f"Vector(x={self.x}, y={self.y})"
```

```python
v1 = Vector(1, 2)

v2 = Vector(3, 4)

result = v1 + v2

print(result)  # Output: Vector(x=4, y=6)
```

In this example, the `__add__` method is defined to return a new `Vector` object with the sum of corresponding components of two `Vector` objects. When `v1 + v2` is called, the `__add__` method is invoked.

4. `__len__` Method:

The `__len__` method is a special method used to return the length of an object. This method is called by the `len` built-in function if present. Here is an example:

```python
```

```python
class CustomList:
    def __init__(self, items):
        self.items = items

    def __len__(self):
        return len(self.items)

    def __str__(self):
        return str(self.items)

custom_list = CustomList([1, 2, 3, 4, 5])
print(len(custom_list))  # Output: 5
```

In this example, the `__len__` method is defined to return the length of the `items` attribute of the `CustomList` object. When `len(custom_list)` is called, the `__len__` method is invoked.

5. `__getitem__` Method:

The `__getitem__` method is a special method used to get the value of an item using square brackets `[]`. Let's take a look at an example:

```python
class CustomList:
    def __init__(self, items):
        self.items = items

    def __getitem__(self, index):
        return self.items[index]

    def __len__(self):
        return len(self.items)
```

```
custom_list = CustomList([1, 2, 3, 4, 5])
print(custom_list[2])  # Output: 3
```

In this example, the `__getitem__` method is defined to return the value of an item at a specific index in the `items` attribute of the `CustomList` object. When `custom_list[2]` is called, the `__getitem__` method is invoked.

6. `__setitem__` Method:

The `__setitem__` method is a special method used to set the value of an item using square brackets `[]`. Let's see an example:

```python
class CustomList:
    def __init__(self, items):
```

```python
        self.items = items

    def __setitem__(self, index, value):
        self.items[index] = value

    def __len__(self):
        return len(self.items)

custom_list = CustomList([1, 2, 3, 4, 5])
custom_list[2] = 10
print(custom_list)  # Output: [1, 2, 10, 4, 5]
```

In this example, the `__setitem__` method is defined to set the value of an item at a specific index in the `items` attribute of the `CustomList` object. When `custom_list[2] = 10` is called, the `__setitem__` method is invoked.

7. `__iter__` and `__next__` Methods (Iterator Protocol):

The `__iter__` and `__next__` methods are special methods used to implement iterators in Python. The `__iter__` method returns an iterator object, and the `__next__` method returns the next item in the iterator. Let's see an example:

```python
class CustomIterator:
    def __init__(self, items):
        self.items = items
        self.index = 0

    def __iter__(self):
        return self
```

```
__next__(self):
    if self.index < len(self.items):
        result = self.items[self.index]
        self.index += 1
        return result
    else:
        raise StopIteration


custom_iterator = CustomIterator([1, 2, 3, 4, 5])
for item in custom_iterator:
    print(item)  # Output: 1, 2, 3, 4, 5
```

In this example, the `CustomIterator` class implements the iterator protocol by defining the `__iter__` and `__next__` methods. The object of this class can be iterated over using a `for` loop.

Conclusion:

Special methods in Python provide a powerful way to customize the behavior of objects and take advantage of object-oriented programming features. By using special methods, you can define how objects of a class interact with built-in functions and operators. This article covered some of the most commonly used special methods in Python and demonstrated how they can be used to create more efficient and intuitive code.

In summary, special methods are an essential part of Python programming and are widely used in many libraries and frameworks. Understanding how to leverage special methods effectively can help you write more expressive and maintainable code in your projects. I hope this article has provided you with a deeper insight into the world of special methods in Python and how they can be used to unlock the power of object-oriented programming.

23. Python Frameworks: Which Ones to Use with Examples

Python is one of the most popular and versatile programming languages in the world. Its simplicity and readability make it an ideal choice for beginners, while its powerful features and vast library of modules make it a favorite among experienced developers. One of the key reasons behind Python's success is its extensive ecosystem of frameworks, tools, and libraries that make development faster, easier, and more efficient.

Frameworks are pre-built structures that provide a foundation for developing applications. They often come with built-in functionalities, libraries, and tools that help developers build web applications, APIs, and more efficiently. They also follow certain conventions and best practices that ensure consistency and maintainability in your code.

In this article, we will explore some of the most popular Python frameworks and discuss their key features, use cases, and examples. Let's dive in!

1. Django

Django is a high-level web framework that encourages rapid development and clean, pragmatic code. It follows the "batteries-included" philosophy, which means that it comes with a wide range of built-in features, including an ORM (Object-Relational Mapper), an admin interface, authentication, and more.

Some key features of Django include:

- Full-featured ORM for interacting with databases

- Built-in user authentication and

authorization

- Admin interface for managing data
- Form handling and validation
- URL routing and view templates

Here's an example of a simple Django web application:

```python
from django.http import HttpResponse

def hello(request):
    return HttpResponse("Hello, world!")
```

2. Flask

Flask is a lightweight and flexible micro-framework that is perfect for small to medium-sized projects. It is easy to get started with Flask, as it has a simple and intuitive API. With Flask, you have the flexibility to choose which libraries and tools you want to use, making it highly customizable.

Some key features of Flask include:

- Lightweight and simple to use

- No boilerplate code

- Built-in development server

- Support for extensions and plugins

Here's an example of a simple Flask application:

```python
from flask import Flask
```

```
app = Flask(__name__)

@app.route('/')
def hello():
    return 'Hello, World!'

if __name__ == '__main__':
    app.run()
```

3. FastAPI

FastAPI is a modern web framework for building APIs with Python 3.6+ based on standard Python type hints. It is highly performant, thanks to the use of the Starlette framework and Pydantic for data validation. FastAPI also provides automatic generation of

OpenAPI documentation, making it easy to test and integrate APIs.

Some key features of FastAPI include:

- Fast performance due to asynchronous programming
- Automatic generation of OpenAPI documentation
- Data validation using Pydantic
- Dependency injection support

Here's an example of a simple FastAPI application:

```python
from fastapi import FastAPI

app = FastAPI()
```

```
@app.get("/")
def read_root():
    return {"Hello": "World"}
```

4. CherryPy

CherryPy is a minimalist web framework that allows you to build web applications with minimal effort. It provides a simple and intuitive API for handling HTTP requests, sessions, and cookies. CherryPy is well-suited for small projects, as it has a low learning curve and requires minimal setup.

Some key features of CherryPy include:

- Minimalistic design

- Built-in HTTP server

- Flexible configuration options

- Session and cookie support

Here's an example of a simple CherryPy application:

```python
import cherrypy

class HelloWorld:
    @cherrypy.expose
    def index(self):
        return "Hello, world!"

cherrypy.quickstart(HelloWorld())
```

5. Pyramid

Pyramid is a flexible and modular web framework that allows you to build applications of any size or complexity. It follows the "pay only for what you eat" philosophy, which means that it is lightweight and doesn't come with unnecessary features. Pyramid provides a range of built-in tools and libraries that make it easy to extend and customize.

Some key features of Pyramid include:

- Flexible and extendable architecture
- Support for various templating engines
- Built-in authentication and authorization
- Extensive documentation and tutorials

Here's an example of a simple Pyramid application:

```python
from wsgiref.simple_server import make_server
from pyramid.config import Configurator
from pyramid.response import Response

def hello(request):
    return Response('Hello, World!')

if __name__ == '__main__':
    config = Configurator()
    config.add_route('hello', '/')
    config.add_view(hello, route_name='hello')
    app = config.make_wsgi_app()
```

```
server = make_server('0.0.0.0', 8000, app)
server.serve_forever()
```

6. Tornado

Tornado is a scalable and non-blocking web framework that is ideal for building real-time web applications. It is asynchronous and event-driven, making it well-suited for applications that require high performance and low latency. Tornado can handle thousands of simultaneous connections, making it perfect for chat rooms, online gaming, and streaming applications.

Some key features of Tornado include:

- Asynchronous and non-blocking I/O
- Websocket support for real-time

communication

- High performance with low latency
- Built-in support for authentication

Here's an example of a simple Tornado application:

```python
import tornado.ioloop
import tornado.web

class MainHandler(tornado.web.RequestHandler):
    def get(self):
        self.write("Hello, world")

def make_app():
    return tornado.web.Application([
```

```
    (r"/", MainHandler),
])


if __name__ == "__main__":
    app = make_app()
    app.listen(8888)
    tornado.ioloop.IOLoop.current().start()
```

These are just a few of the many Python frameworks available for developers. Each framework has its unique features, strengths, and use cases, so it's essential to choose the one that best fits your project requirements and development style. By leveraging the power of these frameworks, you can build robust and scalable applications more efficiently and effectively.

24. Example of Python Application Explained with Examples

Introduction:

Python is a versatile programming language that is widely used in various industries and applications. In this article, we will explore an example of an application built using Python and provide a detailed explanation with code examples.

Example Application:

Let's consider an example of a simple text analysis tool built using Python. This application will take a text input from the user, analyze the text, and provide insights such as word count, character count, and most common words in the text.

Explanation:

To build this text analysis tool, we will use the

following Python libraries:

1. NLTK (Natural Language Toolkit): NLTK is a powerful library for natural language processing tasks such as tokenization, stemming, and tagging.

2. Collections: Collections in Python provides specialized data structures like Counter for counting the frequency of elements.

Code Implementation:

Below is the Python code for our text analysis tool:

```python
import nltk
from nltk.tokenize import word_tokenize
from nltk.corpus import stopwords
from collections import Counter
```

```python
text = input("Enter the text: ")

# Tokenize the text
words = word_tokenize(text)

# Remove stopwords
stop_words = set(stopwords.words('english'))
filtered_words = [word for word in words if word.lower() not in stop_words]

# Count words and characters
total_words = len(filtered_words)
total_characters = sum(len(word) for word in filtered_words)

# Count word frequency
word_freq = Counter(filtered_words)
```

```python
# Find most common words
most_common_words = word_freq.most_common(5)


print("Word Count:", total_words)
print("Character Count:", total_characters)
print("Most Common Words:", most_common_words)
```

In the code above, we first prompt the user to enter the text. We then tokenize the text, remove stopwords, count words and characters, calculate word frequency using Counter, and find the most common words in the text.

Example Usage:

Let's see how our text analysis tool works with an example input:

Input: "Python is a versatile programming language that is widely used in various industries and applications."

Output:

Word Count: 12

Character Count: 84

Most Common Words: [('Python', 1), ('versatile', 1), ('programming', 1), ('language', 1), ('widely', 1)]

Conclusion:

In this article, we explored an example of a text analysis tool built using Python. We leveraged the NLTK library for text processing tasks and the Collections library for counting word frequency. By following the code examples provided, you can create similar applications or even enhance and customize this text analysis tool further.Python is a versatile programming language that is widely used in various industries and applications. In this article, we will explore an example of an application built using Python and provide a detailed explanation with code examples.

Index

1. Introduction to Python programming language pg.4

2. Installing Python on your computer pg.7

3. Basic syntax and data types in Python pg.10

4. Operators and expressions in Python pg.22

5. Control flow statements: if, else, elif, loops in Python pg.31

6. Functions in Python pg.43

7. Data structures: lists, tuples, dictionaries, sets in Python pg.53

8. Variables and Comments in Python pg.68

9. The Python interpreter and the IDLE in Python with examples pg.81

10. File handling in Python pg.87

11. Working with modules and packages pg.98

12. Types of Data in Python with Examples pg.105

13. The functions print and input and Indentation in Python pg.112

14. Numbers and logical operators in Python strings pg.119

15. Dictionary pg.129

16. Set and frozenset are built-in types pg.138

17. Conditional Statements, Loops: for and while in Python pg.143

18. Functions and directives in Python pg.153

19. Error handling and exceptions in Python pg.165

20. Object-oriented programming in Python Working with classes and objects pg.174

21. Exception Handling and File Handling in Python: Managing Modules and Creating New Modules pg.184

22. Special Methods in Python: Unlocking the Power of Object-Oriented Programming pg.193

23. Python Frameworks: Which Ones to Use with Examples pg.207

24. Example of Python Application Explained with Examples pg.220